PRINTHOUSE BOOKS PRESENTS

IT'S WORK, BUT IT'S WORTH IT!
Experiencing God's Best for Your Marriage

Joseph Bryant, Jr., D.Min
VIP INK Publishing Group, Inc.
Atlanta, GA.

Copyright © 2019 Dr. Joseph Bryant, Jr.

ISBN: 978-1-7923-3559-4
Cover designed by SK7

LCCN: 2020935976

Published: 5-15-2020

www.PrintHouseBooks.com

VIP INK Publishing Group; Incorporated
All rights reserved. No parts of this book may be reproduced in any way, shape, or form or by any means without permission in writing from the publisher, or the author, except by a reviewer.

Unless otherwise indicated, Bible quotations are taken from the New International Version of the Bible. Copyright © 2006 by Joseph Bryant Ministries, Inc.

IT'S WORK, BUT *IT'S WORTH IT!*

Experiencing God's Best for Your Marriage

Joseph Bryant, Jr., D.Min

Joseph Bryant, Jr., D.Min
IT'S WORK, BUT IT'S WORTH IT!

"Submit to one another out of reverence for Christ"
Ephesians 5:21

SEMINAR WORKBOOK AND STUDY GUIDE

YOU DESERVE A SUCCESSFUL MARRIAGE!!!

I BELIEVE IN YOUR MARRIAGE!

These are the words I share with every couple that comes to my office looking forward to their wedding day. In a society that is continuously and aggressively opposed to God's biblical blueprint for marriage, with people breaking up over nothing and specializing in making mountains out of molehills, with individuals so selfish they never embrace the idea that "two become one" because they are fighting for "what's mine is mine"—
SOMEBODY'S GOT TO BELIEVE IN MARRIAGE!

These words of encouragement and the study materials that follow are mere morsels of information and inspiration to help couples WORK ON a marriage that is WORTH IT. These renderings in no way are an exhaustive list of "to-dos" for marriage, nor are they a replacement for the enormous amount of concrete advice and anointed insight that God has given through a multitude of counselors, pastors, and couples themselves. The exercises and exhortations come from over seventeen years of marital counseling, particularly the last ten years as a senior pastor, in which I have had numerous opportunities to share a few snippets of insight as we've attempted to construct and reconstruct these precious relationships time and again.

The messages contained in these pages were proclaimed through various venues at the Calvary Hill Community Church of San Francisco (formerly Greater Calvary Hill of Daly City) and in several other arenas where God has allowed me to encourage couples. We were blessed to utilize several of these tools during the workshops and seminars called Marriage Ministry Fellowships held at our church, and the sessions were always tremendously anointed. We've done these trainings with individuals, with couples, with large groups, with laypeople, with ministering couples, and in any other setting where God has given us opportunity. The results then and now continue to assist couples, those who

WANT to be assisted, in repairing, retooling, and rejuvenating their lifelong commitments to one another. The synopsis is simple: If you want your marriage to work, YOU MUST WORK AT IT!

My hope is that every person who picks up this resource will decide their marriage is WORTH THE WORK. None of us is perfect, and we all married imperfect people. Yet there is a "perfection" that is attained when two lives are intertwined to meet the needs of one another, build up one another, and complete one another in ways that could not have been accomplished as a single person. God's plan for marriage still works! God's blueprint for marriage is still the best! God's power for marriage is still available!

May this manual bless your life in reading it as much as it has blessed mine in writing it. May the Lord bless all of you with the incredible marriage He wants you to enjoy!

IT'S WORTH IT!

DEDICATION

This work is dedicated to my beautiful wife, Kelly, who makes my life so precious! You are an incredible woman and an awesome wife, yet words cannot begin to describe what you mean to me.

I am so incredibly grateful for you, and I'm so happy to be married to you. You have truly made my life full and complete. I wouldn't be who I am without you - nor would I want to experience this journey without you!

--I ADORE YOU

ACKNOWLEDGMENTS

To my wonderful parents, Deacon and Mrs. Joseph Bryant, Sr., for giving me life and always encouraging my life. Thank you for showing me the value of staying together and knowing that it TAKES WORK but it is well WORTH IT. Your forty-plus years of marriage are an awesome testimony to me.

To my children, Josiah and Joi, thank you for giving me so much happiness and making me look forward to coming home!

To my friends and mentors, Dr. Alvin C. Bernstine and Dr. Larry W. Ellis, who have shaped all that I am in manhood, ministry, and marriage. I'm forever indebted to you.

To the GOOD NEWS TODAY Team, thanks for pushing me to write, and thanks for making sure that it was all right.

Joseph Bryant, Jr., D.Min
IT'S WORK, BUT IT'S WORTH IT!

To the Marriage Ministry of Calvary Hill, thank you for allowing me the privilege of sharing the joys of the journey with you.

To the Ministerial Couples of Calvary Hill, thank you for opening your lives to me and for reminding me of how much marriage is truly WORTH IT!

To the Calvary Hill Community Church, YOU ARE THE BEST CHURCH IN THE WORLD! Thank you for letting me learn "on the job" how to be a pastor. I LOVE YOU!

HANDBOOK CONTENTS

SECTION ONE: Study Guide

TO HAVE AND TO HOLD

LOVER'S LANES

WE ARE NOT "ALL" CREATED EQUAL

LOVE LANGUAGES

Page. 14

SECTION TWO: Fix-It-Kit

MARRIED, BUT LIVING SINGLE

WORK IT OUT!

7 STEPS TO BEGIN RESTORATION

Page. 52

SECTION THREE: Happily Ever After...

THE 12 MOST IMPORTANT WORDS IN MARRIAGE
(and other sayings)

SUMMARIES & SCRIPTURES

PRAYERS & GOALS

THE MARRIAGE PRAYER

Page. 68

IT'S WORK, BUT IT'S WORTH IT!

SECTION ONE: Study Guide

TO HAVE AND TO HOLD

The Blessing of Marriage
Genesis 2:18-25

MARRIAGE IS THE GREATEST INSTITUTION IN THE WORLD!

Our wonderful God has designed a place for us to have constant companionship, intimate involvement, steady support, and practical partnership through that most intimate of relationships called marriage.

It is through this blessed union that God has planned for us to experience the joys of life together, to create life together, to encourage through life's tough times together, and to know that we are not living life alone – WE ARE TOGETHER. What an incredible reality **to have**; what a precious gift **to hold**.

As with all of God's plans for His people, He has given us a BLUEPRINT that gives us the structure for living out His awesome plan. In the beginning of His great book, the Bible, God completes His week of creation by placing mankind into its appropriate place on this people planet called earth. Here He shares His heart for this jewel of creation and gives mankind a play-by-play description of how and why He designed marriage.

That is why the charge **"to have and to hold"** during the marriage ceremony is a cornerstone to the marriage covenant. The Lord's blueprint is most successful when this phrase enlists the best elements of relationships: commitment, passion, integrity, trust, intimacy, value… just to name a few.

THE BIBLICAL TEXT GIVES US A GREAT PICTURE OF WHAT "To Have and To Hold" looks like:

GOD'S BLUEPRINT FOR MARRIAGE PROVIDES:

"It is not good that man be alone… make a suitable helper" (v. 18)

"She shall be called woman, for she was taken out of man" (v. 23)

___

"For this reason, a man will leave... and cleave" (v. 24)

___

"The two were naked... and not ashamed" (v. 25)

___

TO HAVE AND TO HOLD

<u>LOVE LESSONS</u>
Genesis 2:18-25

SHARING –
"It is not good that man be alone, I will make a <u>suitable</u> helper for him" (one who makes him complete)

_____
_____
_____
_____
_____

STRENGTH –
"She shall be called woman, for she was <u>taken out</u> of man" *(you have what I need, I have what you need)*

_____
_____
_____
_____
_____
_____
_____

SECURITY –

"For this reason, a man will <u>leave… and cleave</u>" (I'm depending on you, you can depend on me)

_____
_____
_____
_____
_____
_____
_____
_____
_____

SAFETY –

"The two were naked and <u>not ashamed</u>" *(I give you all of me; it's no longer a ME thing, it's a WE thing)*

_____
_____
_____
_____
_____
_____
_____

TO HAVE AND TO HOLD

STUDY REVIEW
Genesis 2:18-25

WHAT DOES THE TEXT SAY ABOUT MARRIAGE?

_____
_____
_____
_____
_____
_____
_____
_____

WHAT DOES IT SAY TO THE MAN?

_____
_____
_____
_____
_____
_____
_____
_____
_____

WHAT DOES IT SAY TO THE WOMAN?

_____
_____
_____
_____
_____
_____
_____
_____

WHAT SHOULD WE DO TO "MAKE IT WORK" THIS WAY?

_____
_____
_____
_____
_____
_____
_____
_____

LOVER'S LANES

Understanding Our Roles in the Relationship
Ephesians 5:21-6:4

"Collisions on the road are the result of someone driving in another person's lane. If you want to be safe and successful, STAY IN YOUR LANE – and drive well"
- *Anonymous*

It's hard to have a successful ride in marriage if a husband and wife are confused about which lane they should travel on. Therefore, it becomes extremely important to understand the ROLE that each person in the marriage is given.

God in His wisdom has defined "rules for the road" that help identify the role of a wife and the role of a husband. Once these roles are understood, it provides the framework for maximum fulfillment and love in the marital journey—in THE LOVER'S LANE.

> **The KEY to fulfilling roles in the marital relationship is**
>
> **MUTUAL SURRENDER**
>
> TO GOD AND TO ONE ANOTHER.

"Place yourselves under each other's authority out of respect for Christ" – *Eph. 5:21*

Then, and only then, can the marital roles be appropriately fulfilled. Without surrendering to God, we will fight His purpose and plan for our position in marriage. Without surrendering to our mate, we will not be able to contribute to the relationship what is needed to keep it strong and balanced.

MEN ARE CALLED TO _____

WOMEN ARE CALLED TO _____

*A godly woman will _____ , **IF**
her husband is a man who will
_____ and do whatever it takes
for the good of the family.*

*A godly man will _____ , **IF** his
wife is a woman who will _____
and respect his godly leadership for the
family.*

LOVER'S LANES

LOVE LESSONS
Ephesians 5:21-6:4

1) NEEDS MUST BE MET - verses 28- 29

_____
_____
_____
_____
_____
_____
_____
_____
_____

2) NEVER CREATE DISTANCE - *verse 31*

_____
_____
_____
_____
_____
_____
_____
_____

3) NOTICE GOD'S EXAMPLE - verse 32

4) NURTURE TAKES TIME - verse 33

_____
_____
_____
_____
_____
_____
_____
_____

LOVER'S LANES

STUDY REVIEW
Ephesians 5:21-6:4

WHAT DOES THE TEXT SAY ABOUT MARRIAGE?

_____
_____
_____
_____
_____
_____
_____
_____

WHAT DOES IT SAY TO THE MAN?

_____
_____
_____
_____
_____
_____
_____
_____

WHAT DOES IT SAY TO THE WOMAN?

_____
_____
_____
_____
_____
_____
_____
_____

WHAT SHOULD WE DO TO "MAKE IT WORK" THIS WAY?

_____
_____
_____
_____
_____
_____
_____
_____

WE ARE NOT "ALL" CREATED EQUAL!
Genesis 1:26; 2:18-25 – Proverbs 5:15-23 – Ephesians 5:22-6:4 – 1 Peter 3:1-7

Genesis 1 records in the creation account that God created them "male and female." From the beginning, God has given specific characteristics to each of the genders, although our world tries to erase the line of differentiation. In effect, there *are* things that we acknowledge are unique to each one of the sexes, though there are always exceptions to every rule!

A FEW SIMPLE OBSERVATIONS…

Men were made from the DIRT – so they operate from the outside in
Women were made from inside the body close to the HEART – so they operate from the inside out

Men as boys make nonverbal sounds when they play - usually in the dirt
Women as girls make communication sounds when they play - usually with dolls (people)

Men generally don't communicate their feelings well (they aren't in touch with them like women are)
Women generally communicate their feelings *very* well (which can be overwhelming to men)

Men generally try to let their INTELLECT guide them in making choices
Women generally try to let their EMOTIONS guide them in making choices

Men will often say "I think" when making a statement
Women will often say "I feel" when making a statement

Men were created EXTERNALLY MINDED, so their values and conversations are connected to things external, i.e. – their jobs, sports, politics, tools, cars, etc.
Women were created INTERNALLY MINDED, so their values and conversations are connected to things internal, i.e. – their children, people's feelings, emotional topics, family concerns

Men became MALES because of heightened testosterone in the womb; therefore, SEXUALLY:
Men are usually like microwave ovens
Women are usually like crockpots.

Men often *miss* what is obvious to women
Women often *dismiss* what is important to men

MEN DO NOT SEE THE WORLD LIKE WOMEN
WOMEN DO NOT SEE THE WORLD LIKE MEN

...AND THAT'S OKAY!

Don't expect your mate to be like you – love them for what God made them to be!

WE ARE NOT "ALL" CREATED EQUAL!

LOVE LESSONS

*Genesis 1:26; 2:18-25 – Proverbs 5:15-23
– Ephesians 5:22-6:4 – 1 Peter 3:1-7*

BASIC NEEDS OF MEN

Affirmation

An_____ Wife

Domestic_____

A Recreational_____

Sexual_____

BASIC NEEDS OF WOMEN

Security

A_____ Husband

Domestic_____

A Spiritual_____

Relational_____

HOW TO MEET THE NEEDS OF

_____
_____
_____
_____
_____
_____
_____
_____

LOVE LANGUAGES

Loving my mate where they need to be loved

Everyone loves to be loved, but not everyone receives love in the same way. What may be important to one person may not be so for another. The way one person feels valued and appreciated may be totally different from the way the very person they need validation and appreciation from practices those traits. It's remarkable how many people end up frustrated in marriage, either from assuming they are giving enough love or feeling that they are lacking in love received, simply because of a miscommunication in LOVE LANGUAGE.

LOVE LANGUAGES are the specific ways in which individuals receive love. Other modes may be understood, but only one or two really HIT THE SPOT and make us feel the necessary connection for marital intimacy and happiness. In a very unique way, we usually end up in relationships with people who have a LOVE LANGUAGE that is **totally opposite of our own.** We therefore have to work that much harder to understand what our mate's needs are (since they are SO DIFFERENT from our own), and we have to spend more time explaining to our mate what needs we have ourselves.

FIND YOUR LANGUAGE AND *SHARE IT* - LEARN THEIR LANGUAGE AND *DO IT!*

ACCEPTANCE
Your respect, your commitment, I know where you stand with me

ACTS OF SERVICE
Getting things done: chores, housework, "honey-dos," "baby-dos," etc.

AFFECTION
Physical touch: lots of hugs, holding, etc.

AFFIRMATION
Words or acts of validation; constant encouragement

APPRECIATION GIFTS
Stuff I can touch: presents, surprises, material things

ASSURANCE
Security: relational, emotional; I can be confident in you, I can trust you with me

AVAILABILITY
Quality time; just being together - pay attention to me

LOVE LANGUAGES
Loving my mate where they need to be loved

LOVE LESSONS

<u>Never assume</u> that your mate knows what you need or knows how to give it to you.

Reveal your needs and remind your mate what your "language" is regularly.

Don't be ashamed to teach them how to do it or ask for it to be done when it's not.

Don't take offense when your mate is helping you to love them in the LANGUAGE.

LOVE ISN'T LOVE UNTIL IT REACHES THE ONE I LOVE!

My love languages are:

1. _____

2. _____

3. _____

My mate's love languages are:

1. _____

2. _____

3. _____

HOW TO MEET THE LOVE LANGUAGE OF

_____
_____
_____
_____
_____
_____
_____
_____
_____
_____
_____
_____
_____
_____
_____
_____
_____
_____
_____
_____
_____
_____
_____
_____

IT'S WORK, BUT IT'S WORTH IT!

SECTION TWO: Fix-It-Kit

MARRIED, BUT LIVING SINGLE
Genesis 2:18-25

MARRIAGE IS THE GREATEST INSTITUTION IN THE WORLD… Unfortunately, many people are not enjoying the benefits of this great union because we don't realize one simple truth: You did not get married to live single.

You MAY BE living single:
- *If you can go a whole day without talking to one another and it doesn't cross your mind*
- *If you can be in the same house without enjoying each other's company or prefer to be in another room altogether*
- *If you can go weeks or months without having quality time together and you don't miss it*
- *If you'd rather work than spend time with your spouse*

- *If you regularly make plans for yourself (and your children) without consulting or considering your spouse*
- *If you have things in your life that you do not share or that are "off limits" to your spouse*
- *If you consistently look for opportunities to "leave your spouse" at home when you go where you go*
- *If you talk <u>to</u> and <u>about</u> your mate like an annoying acquaintance more than a precious partner*
- *If you assume what your spouse may do or think, react in anger or frustration, and never give them a chance to share their opinion*
- *If you share more about yourself (your goals, dreams, desires, pains, fears) with coworkers, church members, and others than you do with your spouse*
- *If you still use the words **me**, **my**, and **mine** more than **we**, **us**, and **ours***

WHY BE MARRIED IF ONE CANNOT ENJOY THE BENEFITS OF PARTNERSHIP?
(Why own stock in something you can't reap benefits from?)

HOW CAN THE <u>TWO</u> ENJOY BEING <u>ONE</u> IF <u>ONE</u> HAS DECIDED NOT TO BE <u>ONE</u>?

A lack of intimacy, investment, and involvement with your mate will rob you both

MARRIAGE TAKES WORK – BUT IT'S WORTH IT!

REALITY CHECKS:
- Pain creates distance, unresolved pain creates discord
- Avoiding a conflict only increases the conflict
- Not talking is NOT optional, all talking is not necessary

If your marriage is not what God intended, at least half of your life is out of order, and the other half is miserable.

TAKE TIME TO MAKE TIME
- Once a week have a "simple" date (dinner & a movie, lunch & a walk, long drive & a snack, etc.)
- Once a month do a "special" date (something planned ahead; something to look forward to – concert/sporting event, dress-up dinner, double date, someone's "favorites": food, thing to do, place to go, etc.)
- Once a quarter do something EXTRA special (beach/sightseeing, overnighter/getaway, etc.)
- Once a year, go away together, renew your commitments.

(Ask what THEY need, share what YOU need – talk about where your life IS and where your life is GOING.)

WORK IT OUT!
Doing what it takes to create a peaceful, positive, and pleasing marriage

FOUR MAJOR AREAS OF COUPLE CONFLICT AND MARITAL MADNESS:

1) UNRESOLVED PAST PAIN
(In the relationship, past relationships, or from one's upbringing)

2) UNRECEIVED LOVE LANGUAGE
(I'm not being loved in the way I need to be loved)

3) UNCLEAR COMMUNICATION
(We aren't talking, and when we do, we aren't listening)

4) UNCLEAR, UNMET, OR UNREALISTIC EXPECTATIONS
(This is not what I wanted in my marriage; I thought I had one thing, but…)

DIAGNOSIS – "What is the issue?"

UNRESOLVED PAST PAIN
Confession – why am I like this?
Correction – what do **I need to do** to get over this?

UNRECEIVED LOVE LANGUAGE
What do I need most from my mate?
What do I need to do most for my mate?

UNCLEAR COMMUNICATION
Have I listened to their heart?
Do we talk WITH each other, or do we talk AT each other?

NOT TALKING IS NOT OPTIONAL

UNCLEAR, UNMET, OR UNREALISTIC EXPECTATIONS
I came into this with blinders on.
I didn't want to see what I saw.
I wanted something that I knew wasn't there then, and still isn't there now.
I thought they would change, I thought I could change them.
I thought things would be easier once we got married.

PROGNOSIS – "How do we get it right NOW?"

SUGGESTED REMEDIES FOR:

UNRESOLVED PAST PAIN

- **FORGIVE AND FORGIVE**
  (Stop counting and recounting, and let it go - Matt. 18:22)

- **GET OVER IT FAST**
  (Never let an unaddressed pain live longer than a day – Eph. 4:26)

- **GET HELP IF NEEDED**
  (Seek godly, healthy help - Prov. 11:14)

- **DON'T HOLD YOUR MATE HOSTAGE ANYMORE**

(CHOOSE TO BE HAPPY TOGETHER! – Eph. 5:29)

UNRECEIVED LOVE LANGUAGE

- Figure out what you need. Tell your mate.
- Find out what they need. DO THAT – over and over – and do it well!
- DON'T WAIT UNTIL THEY DO THEIR PART BEFORE YOU DO YOURS
- BE **THE BEST** AT WHAT YOUR MATE WANTS AND NEEDS FROM YOU

UNCLEAR COMMUNICATION

- MAKE NO ASSUMPTIONS
  (assumptions kill relationships)
- RECEIVE, REPEAT, REACT
  (anytime you discuss a serious matter)
- Take 15 minutes to share your day with each other
- Take 5 minutes to pray together daily for the both of you
- Take 1 minute to check in each day when you're apart

UNCLEAR, UNMET, OR UNREALISTIC EXPECTATIONS

- MAKE YOUR MARRIAGE YOUR PRIORITY
(Think: how can **I** bless our marriage today? How can **I** make this a better relationship?)
- ACCEPT WHO YOU MARRIED (don't try to change them, let your heart and God's hand do it!)
- UNDERSTAND **YOUR** ROLE ACCORDING TO **GOD'S WORD**
- PRAY THAT GOD LETS YOU SEE THE BEST IN YOUR MATE ALWAYS
- NEVER, EVER ATTACK YOUR MATE, IN PERSON OR OTHERWISE
- ASK GOD TO CHANGE **YOU** INSTEAD OF ASKING HIM TO CHANGE THEM
- ADMIT YOUR OWN FAULTS BEFORE ACKNOWLEDGING THEIR FAULTS
- DON'T GET DISTRACTED (in thoughts, words, actions, etc. – buried in work, kids, church, other)

- **TEACH YOUR MATE HOW TO LOVE YOU**

MOST OF ALL, <u>PRAY, PRAY, AND PRAY</u> SOME MORE THAT GOD WOULD HEAL THE HURTS OF YOUR PAST, HELP YOU TO FORGIVE PAST PROBLEMS, AND EMBRACE THE PLACE THAT HE WANTS TO TAKE YOU <u>NOW!</u>

7 STEPS IN 7 DAYS TO BEGIN RELATIONSHIP RESTORATION

These recommendations are specially designed for couples who are experiencing a time of conflict, distance, disappointment, and despair in their marriage. May these tools assist you in restoring your marriage to the beautiful relationship God intended you both to have!

7 STEPS (Instructions)

1) No complaints – only compliments

2) No smart remarks – only sweet reminders

3) Pray together in the morning – read together at night

4) Call once a day to share your love – call once a day to share your life (what you are up to that day)

5) Make love on the first day – make love on the last day

6) Have one dream date for him –

have one dream date for her

(i.e. – do something special)

7) Agree to give your best – ask

God to do the rest

*NOTE: If any item is broken, you must start over again with Day One

PREREQUISITES:

Prior to beginning this exercise, write a short paragraph describing your feelings on the following subjects:

YOUR SPOUSE
YOUR HAPPINESS
YOUR FAITH
YOUR BELIEF IN MARRIAGE

Write a prayer to God about what you want Him to do in YOU.

Ask another couple to pray for you before you begin and to be available to you throughout the seven days for accountability, support, encouragement, assistance, etc.

(This should be a couple you trust, one that displays marital and spiritual strengths, and one in which both of you are comfortable with your spouse talking to)

THIS EXERCISE IS NOT MEANT TO UNCOVER OR ERASE THE REALITY OF DEEP-SEATED ISSUES OF PAIN, BETRAYAL, DISTRUST, OR ABUSE. HOWEVER, THESE BEHAVIORS, WHEN COMMITTED TO, CAN CREATE THE POSITIVE ENVIRONMENT, EMOTIONS, AND EXPERIENCES THAT CAN REKINDLE, RECONNECT, AND REFRESH YOUR RELATIONSHIP IN SUCH A WAY THAT YOU BEGIN TO JOURNEY DOWN THE PATH TO WHOLENESS, HEALTH, AND HAPPINESS!

IT'S WORK, BUT IT'S WORTH IT!

SECTION THREE: Happily, Ever After…

12 MOST IMPORTANT WORDS IN MARRIAGE…

I WAS WRONG

I AM SORRY

PLEASE FORGIVE ME

I LOVE YOU

<u>Use these regularly:</u> ***THEY WILL SAVE YOUR MARRIAGE!***

SAYINGS AND STUFF

Don't sweat the small stuff.

Your mate is not that bad, look who they married!

Keep your marriage SAFE – always let your mate be himself or herself.

Never judge their emotions, no matter how CRAZY they seem to you.

Don't let others dictate how you feel about your mate.

Remember the good times.

Never stop dating.

ROMANCE IS FOREVER.

Be the best mate you can be every day!

IT TAKES WORK, BUT IT'S WORTH IT!

Summaries & Scriptures:

GOD MADE MEN TO BE LEADERS: protector and provider for the home (Gen. 2).

A GOOD MAN LEADS BEST BY LISTENING CAREFULLY TO HIS WIFE (1 Pet. 3:7).

GOD MADE WOMEN TO BE NURTURERS: caregivers, the emotional cornerstone of the home. (Titus 2)

A GOOD WOMAN NURTURES BEST BY KNOWING HOW TO TAKE CARE OF THE NEEDS OF HER MATE, HER CHILDREN, AND HERSELF WELL (Prov. 31:10-31).

EVERY MAN **NEEDS** ENCOURAGEMENT, VALIDATION, AND SUPPORT FROM HIS WIFE.
EVERY WOMAN **NEEDS** SECURITY, RESPECT, AND TO BE VALUED BY HER HUSBAND.

COMPROMISE ISN'T ALWAYS 50/50 – it's usually whatever needs to be done to keep the PEACE!

WE ALL LEARN FROM GOOD EXAMPLES. FIND ONE **OR** BECOME ONE.

DON'T LET OUTSIDE FORCES DETERMINE WHAT KIND OF COUPLE YOU ARE, OR WHAT KIND OF MARRIAGE YOU SHOULD HAVE.

NEVER TAKE ADVICE FROM THOSE WHO ARE BITTER.

CONFLICT IS GOD'S REMINDER TO US OF OUR IMPERFECTIONS.

MOST AFFAIRS ARE NOT ABOUT SEX:

THEY ARE THE BYPRODUCT OF SOMEONE'S NEEDS BEING IGNORED *(Not loved in their language, unappreciated, devalued, no communication, etc.).* *THEN SOME OUTSIDER PROVIDES THE DESIRED ATTENTION IN A CONVENIENT WAY.*
PROTECT YOUR MARRIAGE BY PRIORITIZING YOUR MATE'S <u>REAL NEEDS.</u>

MARRIAGE TAKES WORK, BUT IT'S WORTH IT.

PRAYERS AND GOALS

_____
_____
_____
_____
_____
_____
_____
_____
_____
_____
_____
_____
_____
_____
_____
_____

Joseph Bryant, Jr., D.Min
IT'S WORK, BUT IT'S WORTH IT!

Joseph Bryant, Jr., D.Min
IT'S WORK, BUT IT'S WORTH IT!

MARRIAGE PRAYER

*Lord, help us to remember
when we first met
and the strong love
that grew between us.
To work that love into
practical things so nothing
can divide us.*

*We ask for words both
kind and loving
And hearts always ready
to ask forgiveness
as well as forgive.*

*Dear Lord, we put our marriage
into Your hands.
Amen.*

Author Unknown

Pastor Joseph Bryant, Jr.

Joseph Bryant, Jr., D.Min
IT'S WORK, BUT IT'S WORTH IT!

www.PrintHousebooks.com

Joseph Bryant, Jr., D.Min
IT'S WORK, BUT IT'S WORTH IT!

www.ingramcontent.com/pod-product-compliance
Lightning Source LLC
LaVergne TN
LVHW031630070426
835507LV00024B/3415